D1080412

KEEPING SAFE

AROUND ALCOHOL, DRUGS AND CIGARETTES

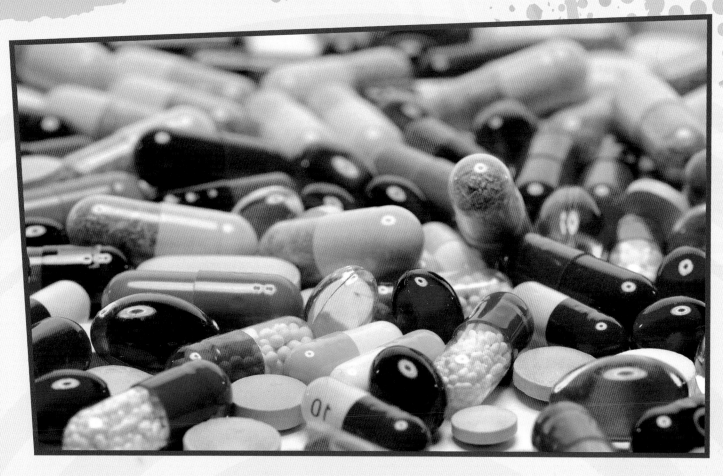

by Anne Rooney

W
FRANKLIN WATTS
LONDON • SYDNEY

First published in 2014 by Franklin Watts

Copyright © Arcturus Holdings Limited

Franklin Watts
338 Euston Road
London NW1 3BH
Franklin Watts Australia
Level 17/207 Kent Street, Sydney NSW 2000

Produced by Arcturus Publishing Limited,
26/27 Bickels Yard, 151–153 Bermondsey Street, London SE1 3HA

Editors: Penny Worms and Joe Harris
Designer: Emma Randall
Cover designer: Emma Randall
Original design concept: Elaine Wilkinson

Picture credits: All images courtesy of Shutterstock except main image page 10,
supplied by iStockphoto.

A CIP catalogue record for this book is available from the British Library.

Dewey Decimal Classification Number 613.6

ISBN 978 1 4451 3249 5

Printed in China

Franklin Watts is a division of Hachette Children's Books,
an Hachette UK company.

www.hachette.co.uk

SL003658UK
Supplier 03, Date 0614, Print Run 3438

CONTENTS

AVOIDING HARM FROM DRINK, DRUGS AND CIGARETTES

At some point, you have probably been around people drinking **alcohol** and smoking cigarettes. You may have also seen people using illegal drugs. Alcohol, cigarettes and drugs have the potential to be dangerous to those using them, and those around them. That's why it's important that you understand the risks involved. The more you know, the better you will be at staying safe and making responsible decisions.

Other young people might encourage you to try alcohol or cigarettes, but you don't have to do what they say.

Alcohol, cigarettes and illegal drugs are all addictive. Although people begin by choosing to use these substances, their bodies can become used to the effects. People sometimes come to depend on drink, cigarettes or drugs, and believe they need them in order to feel happy or even just normal. They cannot give up easily.

SAFETY TIP

You're responsible for your own body, and you have the right and the power to protect it. Stand up for yourself and feel good about yourself by making healthy choices.

At some point, you might feel tempted to try alcohol, cigarettes or drugs. You might be curious, or your friends might put pressure on you to join in. But it's against the law for anyone under 18 years old to buy alcohol or cigarettes, and for anyone to use illegal drugs. It can seriously damage your health, and affect your chances later in life.

It's easy for people of all ages to have fun together in healthy ways without using drink, cigarettes or drugs.

BEING AROUND DRINK, DRUGS AND CIGARETTES

Most young people don't use alcohol, cigarettes or drugs, but that doesn't mean they are not affected by them. You might spend time with family members or friends who smoke, drink too much or use drugs. If they do these things around you, their behaviour may affect you.

People might act differently if they drink too much or use drugs. They might say or do dangerous or upsetting things. Keep yourself safe by staying out of the way of people who are behaving in a dangerous or confusing way.

When adults drink too much, it can be difficult for them to take care of themselves and others.

SAFETY TIP

If you need advice and don't feel you can speak to a parent, ask a responsible adult such as a teacher or school counsellor. They will give you information to help you make good choices. Don't rely on what other people your age tell you.

You might come across cigarette ends or left-over alcoholic drinks in glasses or bottles at home or when you are out. You might even find needles or other evidence of drug use in public places. It's best to leave cigarettes and drinks for adults to clear away. Never touch needles as they can be very dangerous.

People are not allowed to smoke in most public places. This means you can avoid breathing in other people's smoke.

ABOUT ALCOHOL

Many adults drink alcohol in small quantities. They drink because they like the taste, or because it makes them feel sociable and relaxed. However, drinking too much alcohol can be damaging. It is a **depressant**, which means that it can make people feel tired and unhappy. It also slows their reactions.

Adults often drink alcohol at social events like parties.

Some alcoholic drinks are stronger than others, and it's important that people who do drink know how much alcohol they are taking in. **Spirits** such as gin and vodka contain much more alcohol than weaker drinks such as beer. Alcohol is measured in units or by percentage in standard drinks. Most adults keep track of their drinking to stay within safe limits. Drinking small amounts is not harmful for adults, but drinking any alcohol is dangerous for young people.

SAFETY TIP

People who drink above safe limits regularly can do serious harm to their bodies. Alcohol misuse can damage the liver and heart, and cause **cancer**. It can lead to mental-health problems, including **depression**. When **drunk**, people have poor judgement and lose control of their bodies. They might do risky things and have accidents, hurting themselves and others.

There are lots of delicious and exciting drinks that don't contain alcohol.

ALCOHOL AROUND YOU

Being around people who drink too much can be dangerous. They might hurt themselves or someone else – including you – either on purpose or by accident. It's particularly dangerous for someone to drive a car or motorbike after drinking alcohol.

If someone you live with becomes violent after drinking, keep out of their way, and seek help later.

Some people become **aggressive** or violent after drinking too much. Alcohol use is often a cause of **domestic violence**. Sometimes, someone who drinks lashes out at those around them. You don't have to live with domestic violence. Ask for help from a trusted grown-up, such as a teacher or another family member, if someone in your home is violent.

SAFETY TIP

Don't accept a lift in a car from someone who has been drinking alcohol. Ask if someone else can drive instead, or call a parent or another trusted adult for a lift home.

Alcohol often makes people **reckless**. At the same time, it makes it harder for them to control their bodies. They might do dangerous things and perhaps expect you to join in. You aren't being a spoilsport if you refuse – you're being sensible. When the drunk person is **sober** again, they might be embarrassed and glad you didn't join in. They might not remember what they did.

Alcohol is involved in many traffic accidents. Sometimes, people drink so much at night that there is still too much alcohol in their body the next morning for them to drive safely.

ALCOHOL AND YOU

The adult body can deal with alcohol in **moderate** quantities, so adults can drink safely if they follow the advice of health professionals. But while you are young, your brain is still developing and can be permanently damaged by alcohol misuse. Alcohol can cause mental illness and memory problems later, so any amount is dangerous for young people.

If you open a can or bottle yourself, you know the drink is safe.

Drinking too much just once can lead to physical harm. It can make you sick or even cause alcohol poisoning. Severe alcohol poisoning can cause lasting damage to your body. It can even kill you.

Always make sure you know what is in a drink you are offered. Some people think it amusing to 'spike' drinks, adding alcohol without telling someone, but it's dangerous.

Regular misuse of alcohol can poison your liver so that it stops working. That might seem a long time in the future, but more and more people in their twenties are suffering from liver disease caused by alcohol. It also increases the risk of heart disease and some types of cancer, including mouth and throat cancers. And under-age drinkers are more likely to develop **alcoholism** as they get older.

If you drink, you're likely to miss out on schooling or weekend activities because you don't feel well the next day.

CIGARETTES AND ADDICTION

Some adults smoke tobacco in cigarettes, cigars and even pipes. Most smokers say they do it because it makes them feel calm. They might also have fitted smoking into comforting routines – having a cigarette after a meal, for instance. Tobacco is one of the most addictive drugs, and yet it is legal for over 18-year-olds to buy and use it.

'Friends' who try to encourage you to smoke are not really friends.

Two-thirds of people who smoke would like to give up, but because the **nicotine** in tobacco is so addictive, they find stopping very difficult. There is no safe level for smoking – even smoking occasionally is bad for the body. The more someone smokes, and the longer they carry on smoking, the more harm it does to their body.

SAFETY TIP

The best advice is not to start smoking - it's very hard to give up. Studies have shown that nicotine is as addictive as **heroin**, and you can become addicted very quickly.

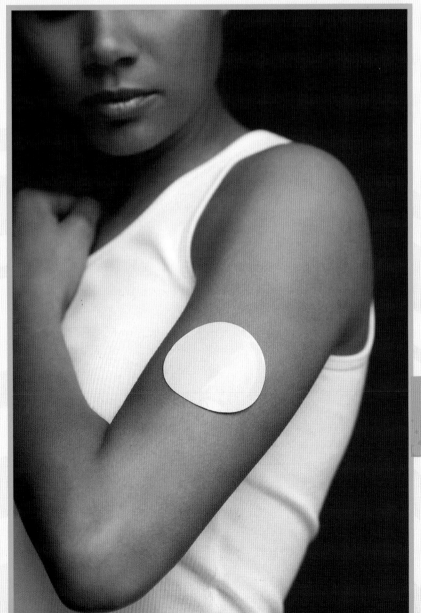

Giving up smoking has immediate benefits. The body starts to repair itself within a few hours of stopping. But it takes a very long time for the body to recover fully, and it might never do so if the smoker has smoked for a long time. There are lots of organizations and products to help people give up smoking. Doctors and school nurses are keen to help.

Special nicotine patches on the skin help people to get used to not smoking.

15

DANGERS OF SMOKING

It is the nicotine in cigarettes that is addictive, but the smoke that damages the body. Smoke contains many poisons. The smoke makes sticky, black **tar**, too, which blocks up the lungs. In young people, smoking stops the lungs growing properly. Smaller lungs take in less air, making it harder for the body to get the oxygen it needs.

Many smokers develop breathing problems and a hacking 'smoker's cough'. Later, they can develop serious lung problems such as lung cancer, bronchitis and emphysema. Three-quarters of smoking-related conditions in smokers affect the lungs. Smoking reduces hunger and the sense of taste, so many smokers don't eat a healthy diet because they don't enjoy food as much.

It's great to be fit and healthy. Smokers are often less fit than non-smokers as smoking makes exercise harder.

The first sign of smoking affecting someone's health is often a cough. Tar from cigarettes quickly harms the lungs.

SAFETY TIP

If you already smoke, you can get help to give up. Talk to any health professional. You won't get into trouble. You can use nicotine patches to help you give up, as it's the smoke, not the nicotine, that causes the harm.

Smoking damages many parts of the body. Smokers suffer more than non-smokers from different types of cancer and from heart disease. There are other unpleasant effects, too – grey, old-looking skin, bad breath, and smelly hair and clothes are not attractive. Also, smokers usually die 13 or 14 years earlier than non-smokers.

AVOIDING SMOKE

Even if you are not a smoker, you can still breathe in smoke from others around you. This is called 'passive smoking'. Many public places are now smoke-free zones, but people can still smoke in their own homes and cars. These places are often where young people are exposed to another person's second-hand smoke.

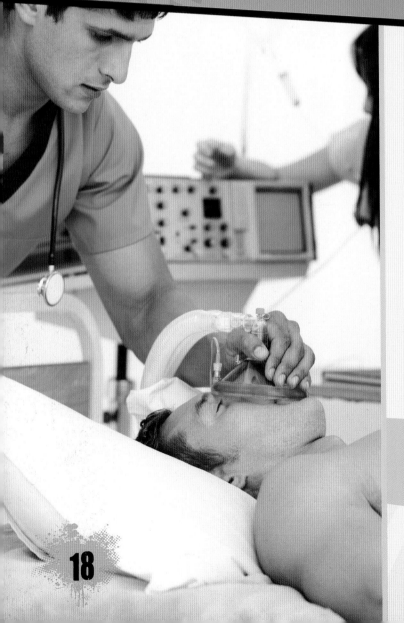

When people smoke in an enclosed space, smoke builds up and affects everyone present, even those who aren't smoking themselves. Passive smoking is not as dangerous as smoking yourself, but it is still harmful. Some people who live with smokers suffer the same illnesses as smokers, even though they don't smoke themselves. Being around smoke is especially dangerous to babies and very young children.

Smoking can lead to very serious health problems, especially for the lungs. This makes it hard to breathe.

SAFETY TIP

If people around you are smoking, go elsewhere or stand as far from them as you can. In your own home, ask people to smoke outside so that the smoke blows away.

Young people sometimes start smoking because it makes them feel grown-up – and then spend years wishing they hadn't started. Others give in to peer pressure (encouragement from others) to try cigarettes and to keep smoking even if they don't really like it at first. Smokers might persuade other people to carry on smoking because it makes them feel better about their own habit, but this is very selfish.

You don't have to smoke just because someone else wants you to – it's your body.

19

ABOUT DRUGS

Drugs are substances that people take to affect their mind or body. They include medicines you take for a headache and illegal drugs such as **cocaine**. Medicines are safe if used properly by the person they are intended for, but it's dangerous to take medicines not given to you by a doctor or parent.

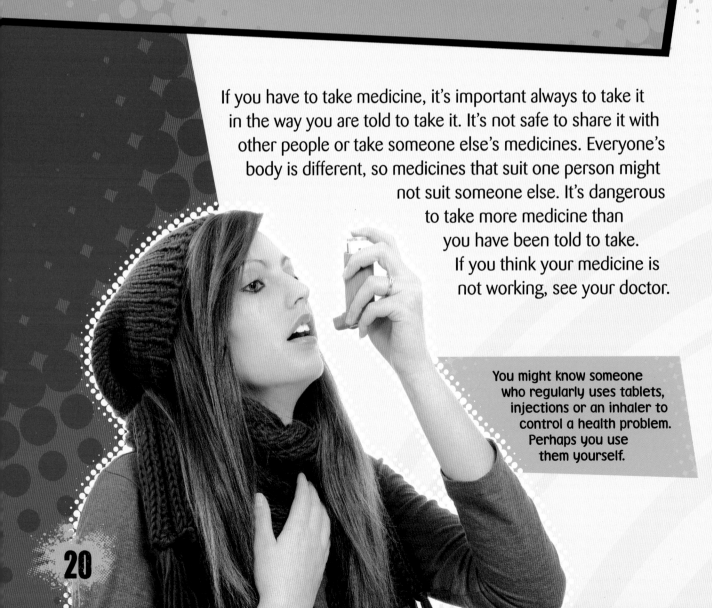

If you have to take medicine, it's important always to take it in the way you are told to take it. It's not safe to share it with other people or take someone else's medicines. Everyone's body is different, so medicines that suit one person might not suit someone else. It's dangerous to take more medicine than you have been told to take. If you think your medicine is not working, see your doctor.

You might know someone who regularly uses tablets, injections or an inhaler to control a health problem. Perhaps you use them yourself.

SAFETY TIP

If you use any medicines yourself, make sure you store them safely. Keep them where any younger brothers or sisters can't find and take them.

Some people use illegal drugs or misuse medicines to experience altered states of mind, usually to feel either calmer or more lively. Even some household substances, such as glue or lighter fuel, are misused to get the same feelings. This can be very dangerous – it's possible to die after using them just once. Don't assume that because a substance is legal it's safe to use in this way.

Misuse of drugs or other substances can lead to illness, poverty and homelessness.

DANGERS OF DRUG MISUSE

Street drugs are illegal substances such as **weed** (marijuana), **MDMA** and cocaine. They are illegal because they are dangerous, and some of them are extremely addictive. They can damage the mind and body, and are particularly harmful for young people who have not finished growing and developing.

Some drug users become so desperate they will do things that seem horrifying, such as sticking unclean needles into their bodies.

People might start to take drugs because they are curious, or because they are unhappy and want something that will make them feel better. But they only feel better for a very short time, and sometimes not at all. As the effects of the drugs wear off, they can feel much worse and want to take the drug again.

SAFETY TIP

Don't pick up dropped needles or cigarette ends, even to put them in a bin. Ask an adult to do it safely. You can catch some deadly diseases from used needles.

Street drugs can affect a person's brain for the rest of their life. Their effects vary depending on the drug. They can cause lasting mental illness, including paranoia (fear for no reason), hallucinations (seeing things that aren't there), depression and memory problems.

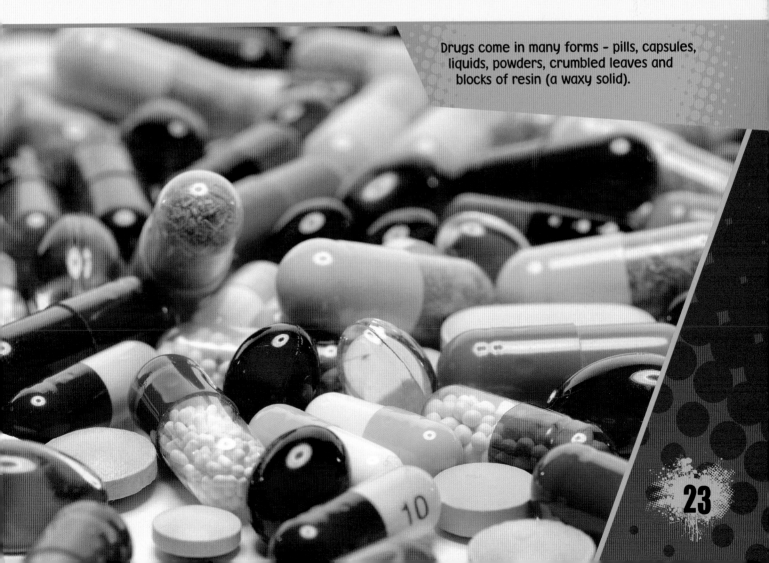

Drugs come in many forms - pills, capsules, liquids, powders, crumbled leaves and blocks of resin (a waxy solid).

23

DANGERS TO YOU

Street drugs are used by some teenagers, so you might come across people who use them or offer them to you. It's best to avoid drug users. If someone offers you drugs, it is best to say no – even using them once can harm you. Keeping your body and mind safe and healthy gives you far more chances to enjoy yourself.

People might start to take drugs because their friends do it, but it becomes a lonely and miserable act later.

Street drugs are not sold in shops, so anyone buying them has to trust an illegal dealer. There is no check on the quality of street drugs. Some are 'cut' (mixed) with other dangerous substances. The people who sell illegal drugs are not interested in the safety of the people who buy the drugs.

SAFETY TIP

Drugs affect people differently. You might know someone who uses drugs and doesn't seem badly affected but that doesn't mean you will react in the same way to the same drugs. And you can't see the long-term effects the drugs are having.

Street violence and gang activity are often related to drug dealing. It's a very dangerous world to get mixed up in. As well as the risk of harm, street drugs are illegal. Anyone who takes them can get into trouble with the police. The police will tell your parents and school if you are found carrying or using drugs.

Taking pills or smoking weed won't really help with feeling miserable. It's better to talk to someone, or take some exercise, which is proven to give you a positive boost.

TAKING A STAND

An important part of looking after yourself is knowing you have a right to a good and healthy life. Sometimes, you might feel awkward standing up to people, but it's good to do it. They should respect your rights and wishes, but you have to show them you respect yourself.

If people around you smoke or use alcohol in a way that affects you badly, you need to speak out. It's important that you do this, even though it may be hard. Tell a parent, relative or other trusted adult how the behaviour makes you feel. You could ask for support from your doctor, or a teacher or counsellor at school.

It takes courage to ask for help with a problem - but it's well worth it as sorting things out will make your life better.

SAFETY TIP

If you already have a problem with drink, drugs or cigarettes, your doctor or a counsellor at school will help you to deal with it. They won't judge you or cause trouble for you, so don't be afraid to get help.

Some people your own age might encourage you to try cigarettes, drink or drugs. They might try to make you feel cowardly or left out if you don't join in. Say something like 'No thanks, I'm fine,' or 'I don't like to do that stuff, thanks.' True friends won't try to force you.

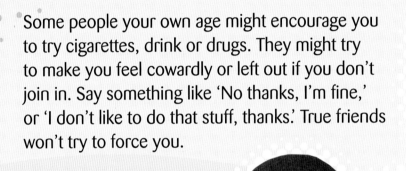

There are lots of people who can help you with problems - you don't have to struggle alone.

SUMMARIZER

Here's a reminder of the most important points made in the book. Look back if you want to see more information about anything.

1 If you know about the dangers from alcohol, cigarettes and drugs, you are in a good position to look after yourself and make healthy choices.

2 Alcohol can damage the brain, liver and other parts of the body if used too much or by younger people.

3 Alcohol can lead people to make foolish choices or act dangerously – make sure they don't endanger you.

4 Cigarettes are very damaging to the lungs and other parts of the body.

5 Cigarettes are extremely addictive, and there is no safe level of use.

6 Breathing in second-hand smoke (passive smoking) is dangerous.

7 Illegal street drugs are very dangerous and buying them can get you involved with criminal and violent people.

8 Breaking the law to buy alcohol, cigarettes or drugs can lead to trouble with the police that affects your chances later in life of going to college or getting a job.

9 If you have a problem with someone around you using drink, cigarettes or drugs, you can get help.

10 If you have a problem yourself with drink, cigarettes or drugs, your doctor or school counsellor can help you to get treatment without getting into trouble.

11 Stand up for yourself! You have a right to healthy surroundings and a healthy start in life.

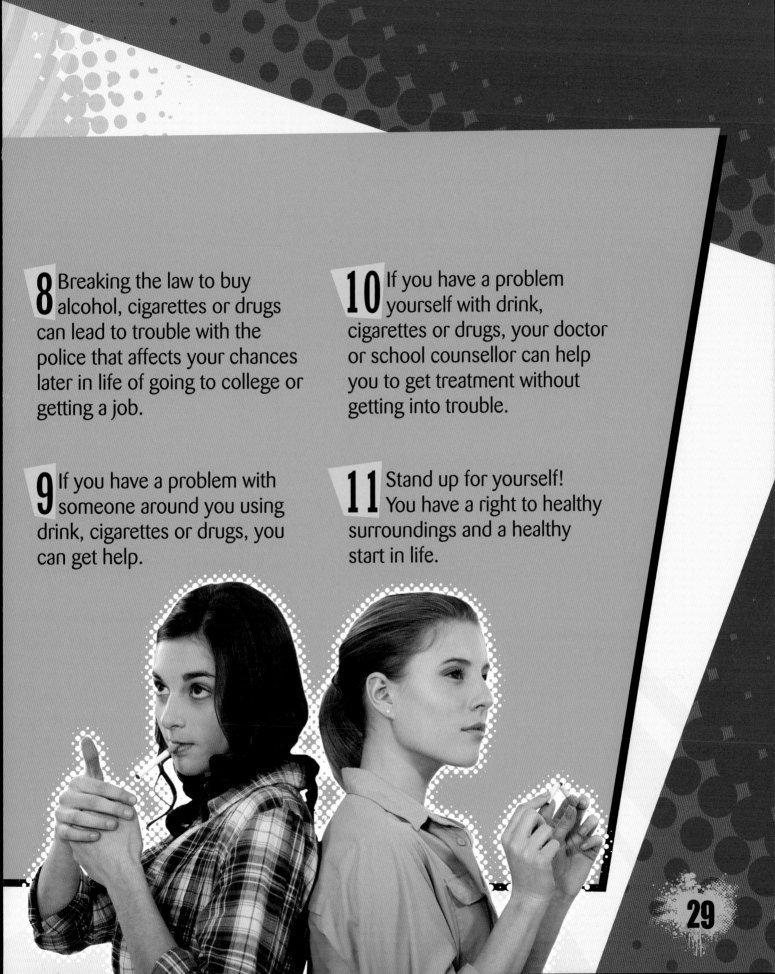

GLOSSARY

addicted unable to stop doing something

aggressive angry, and behaving in a threatening way

alcohol a colourless liquid in some drinks, such as beer, wine and spirits, that can make a person lose control over their mind and body

alcoholism to be so dependent on the effects of alcohol that you have to keep drinking it, even if you don't want to

cancer a serious disease caused when a person's cells develop in the wrong way and which can then spread

cocaine a powerful and addictive drug used in medicines, but also used illegally by people who like the way it affects their mind

depressant something that lowers your spirits and makes you feel less happy

depression a serious condition when a person feels sad and without hope, often making them unable to live normally

domestic violence when there is violence between family members within the home

drunk when a person has drunk so much alcohol that it affects the way they speak, move and behave

heroin an extremely dangerous and addictive drug, used in medicine but also used illegally

MDMA (sometimes known as ecstasy) a drug used illegally by people who like the way it makes them feel but it can have dangerous effects

moderate an average amount; not too much

nicotine the poisonous chemical in tobacco that is so addictive that smokers find it difficult to stop smoking

reckless without any care for your own safety or the safety of others

sober the opposite of 'drunk'; to be free from alcohol or drugs

spirits strong alcoholic drinks, such as vodka, gin, whisky and rum

tar a sticky substance in tobacco smoke

weed (also known as marijuana or cannabis) the dried leaves of the hemp plant that are smoked as an illegal drug

FURTHER INFORMATION

Websites

www.drugs.health.gov.au/internet/drugs/publishing.nsf/content/youth
Help with resisting pressure to try drugs, and information about drugs and their effects

www.getthelowdown.co.uk/
Health website for young people that includes information on how alcohol, cigarettes and drugs affect the body and mind

www.nhs.uk/Livewell/smoking
The National Health Service website that has a specific section for under 18s on why you should quit smoking and how

www.quitbecause.org.uk/
Help with quitting smoking, especially for people aged 8 to18

www.talktofrank.com/
Information about all types of drugs, and what to do if you want help yourself or want help for a friend

www.thecoolspot.gov/right_to_resist.asp
How to stand up to people who try to persuade you to do something you don't want to do

Books

Alcohol (Teen FAQs), **Anne Rooney**, Franklin Watts, 2010

Drinking and Smoking (Know the Facts), **Paul Mason**, Wayland, 2008

Drugs (Teen FAQs), **Anne Rooney**, Franklin Watts, 2010

Smoking (How Can I Be Healthy?), **Sarah Ridley**, Franklin Watts, 2011

Helplines

(UK) Childline 0800 1111
Free telephone helpline giving support with problems of all types, including family members harming you after using drink or drugs, and problems of your own with drink, cigarettes or drugs. The phone number won't show up on your phone bill. www.childline.org.uk

(Australia) Kids' Helpline 1800 55 1800
Free phone or online counselling with a personal counsellor.
www.kidshelp.com.au/teens/get-help/web-counselling/

Samaritans 08457 90 90 90
A telephone helpline run by volunteers who are there to listen to your problems and help you with your feelings

INDEX

SERIES CONTENTS

Keeping Safe around Alcohol, Drugs and Cigarettes
- Avoiding Harm from Drink, Drugs and Cigarettes
- Being Around Drink, Drugs and Cigarettes
- About Alcohol • Alcohol Around You • Alcohol and You
- Cigarettes and Addiction • Dangers of Smoking
- Avoiding Smoke • About Drugs • Dangers of Drug Misuse
- Dangers to You • Taking a Stand

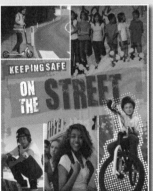

Keeping Safe on the Street
- Be Street Smart • Know Your Journey
- Stay Aware • Dog Dangers • Stranger Danger
- Trouble on the Streets • Safe Cycling
- Safe Skateboarding • Keep Away from Building Sites
- Keep Away from Rail Tracks
- Stay Safe on Public Transport • After Dark

Keeping Safe Online
- Having a Happy Online Life • Cyberbullying
- Using Social Media Safely • Share Carefully
- Keep Your Information Safe • Online Chat
- Stay in Your Comfort Zone • Too Much
- Click With Care • Going Viral • Infected Computer
- Dealing With Problems

Keeping Safe with Friends and Family
- Making Decisions • Helping Out • Emergency!
- Anger and Arguments • Family Matters • Pet Safety
- Peer Pressure • Safety at Home • Out with Friends
- Going to Friends' Houses • Your Body Belongs to You
- Good Secrets and Bad Secrets